UNCOVERING THE PAST:
ANALYZING PRIMARY SOURCES

NUCLEAR WEAPONS AND THE ARMS RACE

T4-AEE-866

HEATHER HUDAK

CRABTREE
PUBLISHING COMPANY
WWW.CRABTREEBOOKS.COM

Author: Heather C. Hudak
Editor-in-Chief: Lionel Bender
Editors: Simon Adams, Ellen Rodger
Proofreaders: Laura Booth, Wendy Scavuzzo, Anastasia Suen, Angela Kaelberer
Project coordinator: Petrice Custance
Design and photo research: Ben White
Production: Kim Richardson
Production coordinator and prepress technician: Ken Wright
Print coordinator: Katherine Berti
Consultant: Amie Wright, The New York Public Library

Produced for Crabtree Publishing Company by Bender Richardson White

Photographs and reproductions:
Alamy: 13 (John Frost Newspapers), 38–39 (Shingo Ito/AFLO/Alamy Live News); Getty Images: 4–5 (Universal Images Group), 7 (Cornell Capa), 8–9 (MPI), 11 (Hulton Archive), 16–17 (Corbis Historical), 22 (Los Alamos National Laboratory), 23 Btm (New York Daily News Archive), 27, 33 (Corbis), 29, 34–35 (Bettmann), 30 (Hulton Archive), 32 (Carl Mydans), 40–41 (Raveendran), 41 (Kyodo News); Last Gasp Publishers: 15 Btm (Keiji Nakazawa, Cover design by Evan Hayden); Library of Congress: Top Left (Icon) 4, 6 (LC-DIG-ds-02944), 4 (LC-USZ62-39852), 21 (LOC HAER COLO,30-GOLD.V,1—13); Shutterstock : 1 (John Wollwerth), 3 (ID1974), Top Left (Icon) 8, 10, 12, 14 (Allen J. M. Smith), 12 (chuugo), 15 Top (bissig), Top Left (Icon) 16, 18 (Sergey Kamshylin), Top Left (Icon) 20, 22, 24, 26, 28, 30, 32 (gerasimov_foto_174), Top Left (Icon) 34, 36 (BestPhotoPlus), Top Left (Icon) 38, 40 (Rena Schild); Topfoto : 6–7, 36 (World History Archive), 10, 20–21 (The Image Works), 14 (Ronald Grant Archive), 18, 19 (The Granger Collection), 24 (HIP), 25 (TASS), 26 (Topham), 28–29 (Roger Viollet), 31 (Topfoto), 37 (Ullsteinbild); wikimedia.org: front cover, 35, 23 Top
Map: Stefan Chabluk
Cover: Henry A. Kissinger helped negotiate limitations on nuclear arms worldwide as head of the U.S. National Security Council. He later became Secretary of State for the United States.

Library and Archives Canada Cataloguing in Publication

Hudak, Heather C., 1975-, author
Nuclear weapons and the arms race / Heather Hudak.

(Uncovering the past: analyzing primary sources)
Includes bibliographical references and index.
Issued in print and electronic formats.
ISBN 978-0-7787-4801-4 (hardcover).--
ISBN 978-0-7787-4827-4 (softcover).--
ISBN 978-1-4271-2090-8 (HTML)

1. Nuclear weapons--History--Juvenile literature. 2. Nuclear weapons--History--Sources--Juvenile literature. 3. Arms race--History--20th century--Juvenile literature. 4. Arms race--History--20th century--Sources--Juvenile literature. I. Title.

U264.H83 2018 j355.02'17 C2017-907717-1
C2017-907718-X

Library of Congress Cataloging-in-Publication Data

CIP available at the Library of Congress

Crabtree Publishing Company
www.crabtreebooks.com 1-800-387-7650

Printed in the U.S.A./022018/CG20171220

Copyright © **2018 CRABTREE PUBLISHING COMPANY**. All rights reserved. No part of this publication may be reproduced, stored in a retrieval system, or be transmitted in any form or by any means, electronic, mechanical, photocopying, recording, or otherwise, without the prior written permission of Crabtree Publishing Company. In Canada: We acknowledge the financial support of the Government of Canada through the Canada Book Fund for our publishing activities.

Published in Canada
Crabtree Publishing
616 Welland Ave.
St. Catharines, ON
L2M 5V6

Published in the United States
Crabtree Publishing
PMB 59051
350 Fifth Avenue, 59th Floor
New York, NY 10118

Published in the United Kingdom
Crabtree Publishing
Maritime House
Basin Road North, Hove
BN41 1WR

Published in Australia
Crabtree Publishing
3 Charles Street
Coburg North
VIC, 3058

R0452847088

UNCOVERING THE PAST

INTRODUCTION: THE PAST COMES ALIVE....4
The Cold War between the United States and the Soviet Union after World War II, and how it developed into the Nuclear Arms Race.

HISTORICAL SOURCES: TYPES OF EVIDENCE....8
The two main types of historical evidence—primary sources and secondary sources—and how to distinguish them; the importance of visual and auditory sources.

ANALYZING EVIDENCE: INTERPRETATION....16
Analyzing evidence to determine if a source is credible; the importance of analyzing bias.

THE STORY UNCOVERED: THE NUCLEAR ARMS RACE....20
The discovery of nuclear fission in 1938 and the subsequent nuclear arms race; the first three bombs in 1945; nuclear testing in the 1950s.

DIFFERENT VIEWS: SLOW IT DOWN....34
The steps taken by the United States, the Soviet Union, and other nations since 1963 to limit the spread of nuclear weapons and their testing.

MODERN EXAMPLES: HISTORY REPEATED....38
The current nuclear arms race between India and Pakistan, and the recent development of nuclear weapons by North Korea.

Timeline....42
Bibliography....44
Internet Guidelines....45
Glossary....46
Index....48

THE PAST COMES ALIVE

"The nuclear arms race is like two sworn enemies standing waist deep in gasoline, one with three matches, the other with five."

American astronomer and author Carl Sagan, 1983

The Arms Race was an event that happened in the recent past. Following the discovery of **nuclear fission** in the late 1930s, U.S. scientists began working on a weapon that tapped its power. At the same time, **World War II** was raging in Europe. Many believed an **atomic** weapon was needed to win the war.

The first nuclear bomb was tested in New Mexico on July 16, 1945. A few months later, although the war in Europe was now over, the war against Japan still continued in the Pacific. In order to end that war, U.S. President Harry S. Truman ordered atomic bombs to be dropped on the cities of Hiroshima, Japan, on August 6, and on Nagasaki, Japan, on August 9. The results were **catastrophic**.

Following World War II, scientists in the United States and the Soviet Union continued to work on nuclear weapons technology. At the same time, tensions rose between the two nations. Both countries had vastly different political systems and each believed their own to be the best. This time of tension is known as the **Cold War**, which lasted from 1946 to 1991.

The United States was increasingly worried about the threat of **communism**. It decided a strategy of **containment** was the best defense. In order to contain potential Soviet expansion, the United States would need to fight fire with fire. To ensure it was ready to fight if the time came, the country began stockpiling arms and developing new atomic weapons. It wasn't long before the Soviets started doing the same. The Arms Race had officially begun.

▲ The atomic bomb dropped on Nagasaki, Japan, resulted in more than 50,000 deaths, another 50,000 casualties, and a column of dust and debris that rose 45,000 feet (13,716 m) into the air.

DEFINITIONS

The **Union of Soviet Socialist Republics** (U.S.S.R.) was a communist country in Northern Asia and Eastern Europe that was made up of Russia and 14 other countries.

Soviet is a term used to describe anything related to the U.S.S.R.

Communism refers to an economic and political system in which all property is owned by its members and is used for the good of all people.

Capitalism refers to an economic and political system in which trade and industry are privately owned.

◀ About 70 percent of the buildings in Hiroshima, Japan, were destroyed by the atomic bomb dropped on the city in August 1945.

EVIDENCE RECORD CARD

Hiroshima leveled by atomic bomb

LEVEL Primary source
MATERIAL Photograph
LOCATION Japan
DATE March 1946
SOURCE Getty Images

THE START OF THE ARMS RACE

In 1917, after **centuries** of **imperial** rule that had led to great poverty, the Russian people rose up. It resulted in a revolt, the Russian Revolution, and the establishment of a new economic system—communism—in which the country's wealth was shared equally among all its citizens. The communist government became very powerful. By 1922, the old Russian Empire became the Soviet Union. The United States, by contrast, had a capitalist system. In it, most of the country's wealth and property were privately owned. Personal freedom and **democracy** were important. Many Americans feared the spread of communism to the United States.

With the horrors of Hiroshima and Nagasaki still fresh in people's minds, the world's top nuclear scientists warned of the dangers if too much atomic power was placed in the hands of any one government. Immediately after World War II ended, the United Nations proposed **disarmament** of all nuclear weapons and a method for regulating nuclear activities through the United Nations Atomic Energy Commission.

PERSPECTIVES

Look at the Soviet **propaganda** shown here. What point of view does it represent? What does it tell us about how the Soviets felt about the Americans at the time?

▶ **Soviet propaganda included posters that warned the United States against developing nuclear weapons technology.**

"Somehow we must transform the dynamics of the world power struggle from the negative nuclear arms race which no one can win to a positive contest to harness man's creative genius for the purpose of making peace and prosperity a reality for all of the nations of the world."

Martin Luther King, Jr., receiving the Nobel Peace Prize at the University of Oslo, December 11, 1964

On June 14, 1946, the United States, with the support of Great Britain and Canada, proposed the Baruch Plan. Under this plan, the United States would hand over its atomic weapons provided all other countries agreed not to produce similar weapons. An international inspection agency would regulate future atomic activities. The Soviet government rejected this plan, believing the system was **biased** toward the United States. Instead, they countered with the Gromyko Plan. This called for the United States to destroy all its nuclear weapons, which the U.S. government promptly rejected. In the meantime, the Soviets started developing their own atomic weapons, which they first tested in August 1946.

The Soviet Union forged ahead with plans to build more powerful nuclear weapons, with the Americans eager to outdo their Soviet rivals. By the 1950s, the Cold War escalated to a boiling point. This time in history is known as the Arms Race.

ANALYZE THIS

What reason did the Soviets have for rejecting the Baruch Plan? Why did the Americans dislike the Gromyko Plan?

▼ Soviet ambassador to the United Nations Andrei A. Gromyko (left), British ambassador to the United Nations Alexander Cadogan (center), and U.S. diplomat Bernard Baruch (right) at the atomic energy meeting in October 1946.

TYPES OF EVIDENCE

"Our world faces a crisis as yet unperceived by those possessing power to make great decisions for good or evil. The unleashed power of the atom has changed everything save our modes of thinking and we thus drift toward unparalleled catastrophe."

The New York Times, May 25, 1946

Historians are people who study the past. They look for sources of information that provide **evidence** about events that happened some time ago. They **analyze** and interpret these sources. In order to study the past, historians need to look at the causes of events and their effects on **society** and **culture**. Since there is no way for historians to go back in time and experience it themselves, they look for evidence that helps them see it through the eyes of the people who were there. Evidence, or proof, consists of any objects, statements, facts, or information. Historians use this evidence to learn about the culture, beliefs, and **economy** of the time and draw conclusions about it.

There are four main types of evidence. Written evidence includes letters, receipts, books, and other documents. If you keep a diary or send emails to friends, future historians can use them to learn about life in the 21st century. Images you post on Instagram are a form of visual evidence. Drawings, maps, and video footage are other examples. Oral evidence refers to anything that is heard aloud such as music, speeches, and audio recordings. Objects, like statues, clothing, and tools, are types of physical evidence. There is plenty of evidence from the Arms Race that historians can use to find out about the beliefs and culture of that period in time.

▶ On August 2, 1939, the physicist Albert Einstein sent a letter to President Franklin D. Roosevelt alerting him to the discovery of nuclear energy in Germany and its potential use as a weapon.

▶ On December 2, 1942, a group of scientists in Chicago, Illinois, achieved the first-ever self-sustaining nuclear reaction, thereby initiating the controlled release of nuclear energy. The reactor consisted of lumps of **uranium** and uranium oxide placed inside blocks of graphite.

Albert Einstein
Old Grove Rd.
Nassau Point
Peconic, Long Island

August 2nd, 1939

F.D. Roosevelt,
President of the United States,
White House
Washington, D.C.

Sir:

Some recent work by E.Fermi and L. Szilard, which has been communicated to me in manuscript, leads me to expect that the element uranium may be turned into a new and important source of energy in the immediate future. Certain aspects of the situation which has arisen seem to call for watchfulness and, if necessary, quick action on the part of the Administration. I believe therefore that it is my duty to bring to your attention the following facts and recommendations:

In the course of the last four months it has been made probable - through the work of Joliot in France as well as Fermi and Szilard in America - that it may become possible to set up a nuclear chain reaction in a large mass of uranium,by which vast amounts of power and large quantities of new radium-like elements would be generated. Now it appears almost certain that this could be achieved in the immediate future.

This new phenomenon would also lead to the construction of bombs, and it is conceivable - though much less certain - that extremely powerful bombs of a new type may thus be constructed. A single bomb of this type, carried by boat and exploded in a port, might very well destroy the whole port together with some of the surrounding territory. However, such bombs might very well prove to be too heavy for transportation by air.

PRIMARY SOURCES

Source materials are the main types of evidence historians use to uncover the past. A source material is an **artifact** that was created during or about the time of an event a historian is studying. It can include a news article, recording, book, photograph, painting, blog post, or object. We find source materials in libraries, digital databases, **archives**, museums, and on trusted Internet sites.

The most important types of evidence historians look for are **primary sources**. These are firsthand accounts by people who personally witnessed or took part in events at the time they occurred. If you've ever observed a car accident and then had to give a statement to the police, your account is a primary source. Other types of primary sources include diaries, letters, creative writings, transcripts, surveys, statistical data, lab reports, objects, and memos.

There are many different types of primary source materials about the Arms Race. Nuclear scientists, such as Albert Einstein and Enrico Fermi, wrote autobiographies that detailed their personal experiences developing nuclear technology. There are many pieces of correspondence, such as letters and memos written by key scientists, military leaders, and politicians in the Arms Race, including President Harry S. Truman, Julius Robert Oppenheimer, and General Douglas

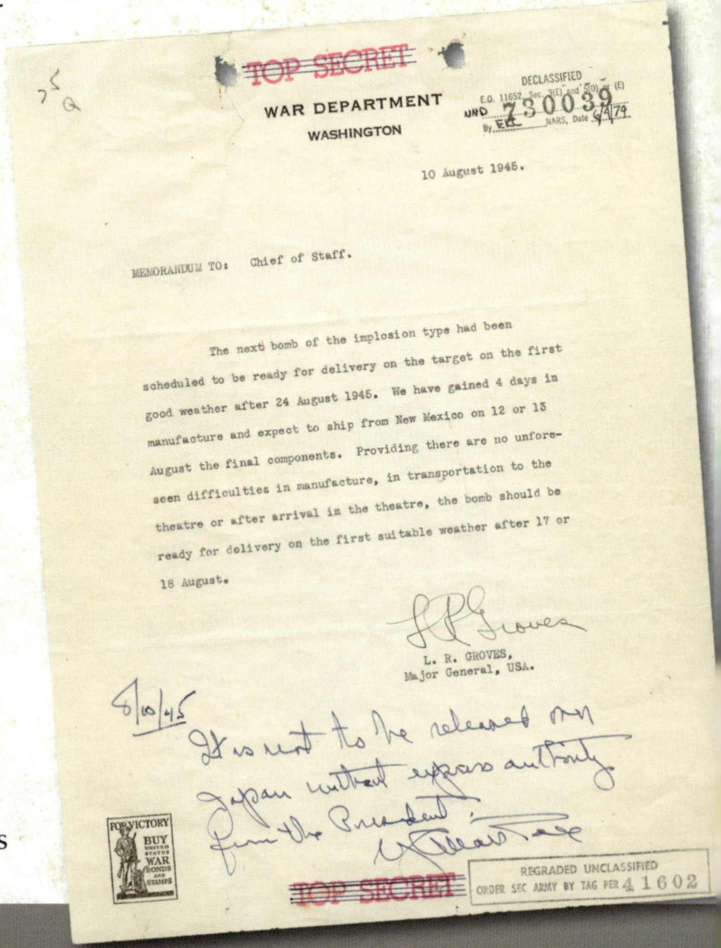

TOP SECRET

DECLASSIFIED
E.O. 11652, Sec. 3(E) and 5(D) or (E)
NND 730039
By EC NARS, Date 4/4/79

WAR DEPARTMENT
WASHINGTON

10 August 1945.

MEMORANDUM TO: Chief of Staff.

The next bomb of the implosion type had been scheduled to be ready for delivery on the target on the first good weather after 24 August 1945. We have gained 4 days in manufacture and expect to ship from New Mexico on 12 or 13 August the final components. Providing there are no unforeseen difficulties in manufacture, in transportation to the theatre or after arrival in the theatre, the bomb should be ready for delivery on the first suitable weather after 17 or 18 August.

L. R. Groves

L. R. GROVES,
Major General, USA.

8/10/45
It is not to be released on Japan without express authority from the President.
GCMarshall

FOR VICTORY BUY UNITED STATES WAR BONDS AND STAMPS

TOP SECRET

REGRADED UNCLASSIFIED
ORDER SEC ARMY BY TAG PER 41602

"For only when our arms are sufficient beyond doubt can we be certain beyond doubt that they will never be employed."
John F. Kennedy

▲ On August 10, 1945, General Groves, director of the **Manhattan Project** producing the first atomic bombs, sent a memo to George Marshall, U.S. Army Chief of Staff, saying the next atomic bomb would be ready to drop on Japan in less than a week. President Truman called off the bombing, which Marshall noted at the foot of the memo.

MacArthur. Copies of **treaties** and laws related to nuclear weapons are available to analyze, too.

Many primary sources were not readily available to the public at the time they were created. In North America they included **confidential** information that the U.S. and Canadian governments did not want to fall into the wrong hands, such as Soviet scientists and **spies**. Today, many of these sources can be accessed by anyone. An example is the "Preliminary Statement of the Association of Manhattan District Scientists," written by Irving Kaplan and Francis Bonner on behalf of the many scientists who were working on nuclear technology for the U.S. government. Written at the start of the Cold War, the statement urges the government to reduce the secrecy surrounding nuclear projects.

PERSPECTIVES

What questions does this magazine article raise in your mind? Where can you find answers to your questions? Based on what you see, list a few things you might infer from the article.

Has Russia the Atom Bomb?

BY HANSON W. BALDWIN
Military Analyst, New York Times;
Graduate, U. S. Naval Academy

DOES Russia have the atom bomb?

Soviet Foreign Minister Molotoff and his mouthpiece Vishinsky have stated that the Russians know the "secret" of the bomb.

They undoubtedly do, but that does not mean that Russia has been able to build a bomb. In my opinion they have not produced an atomic bomb to date of writing—but they will. Intelligence information—unofficial and inconclusive but indicative—says "no bomb yet."

Our own experience in manu- [*Continued on page 62*]

60 *Mechanix Illustrated*

▶ **Military editor Hanson W. Baldwin of *The New York Times* wrote an article entitled "Has Russia the Atom Bomb?" for the March 1948 issue of *Mechanix Illustrated*, a do-it-yourself magazine of the time.**

VISUAL SOURCES

Some sources of evidence are visual. They include images, posters, paintings, and newsreels. Primary visual sources are created as events take place. They include videos and photographs of actions and people. In the case of the Arms Race, there are many photographs of bombs being tested, as well as political cartoons that were featured in U.S. newspapers. Soviet propaganda was distributed across the U.S.S.R. to help promote pride in the nation and its superior nuclear technology.

Because the Arms Race was fairly recent, people used cameras and other recording devices to capture events live. There are also drawings and diagrams that scientists made of nuclear weapons. Physical objects of the race, such as **missiles**, bombs, and test sites, are also examples of primary visual sources.

Visual sources give us a unique **perspective** of history that we can't find in other types of evidence. They allow us to see for ourselves what life and society were like during a specific period in time. How did people dress? What types of cars did they drive? How were different **classes** shown? When we read a book or listen to a recording, we can't see the expression on a person's face.

▼ **Hiroshima Peace Memorial Park in the center of Hiroshima is a UNESCO World Heritage Site that contains several memorials to the victims of the 1945 atomic bombing.**

Photographs, paintings, and newsreels give us insight into how people were feeling and reacting to events.

Auditory sources are another important type of source materials historians use to study the past. Songs and instrumental music are examples of auditory source materials. During the Arms Race, people used recording devices to capture live speeches and radio interviews with scientists like Albert Einstein and Julius Robert Oppenheimer. There are recordings of John F. Kennedy's address to the United Nations in 1961 in which he calls for an end to the Arms Race.

Like visual sources, auditory sources give us a unique glimpse into history. We can hear happiness or sadness in people's voices as they speak. We can hear the roar of a cheering crowd and the powerful bang of an explosion when a bomb hits its target.

▼ On August 7, 1945, headlines on newspapers around the world, such as *The New York Times*, told of the bombing in Hiroshima the day before.

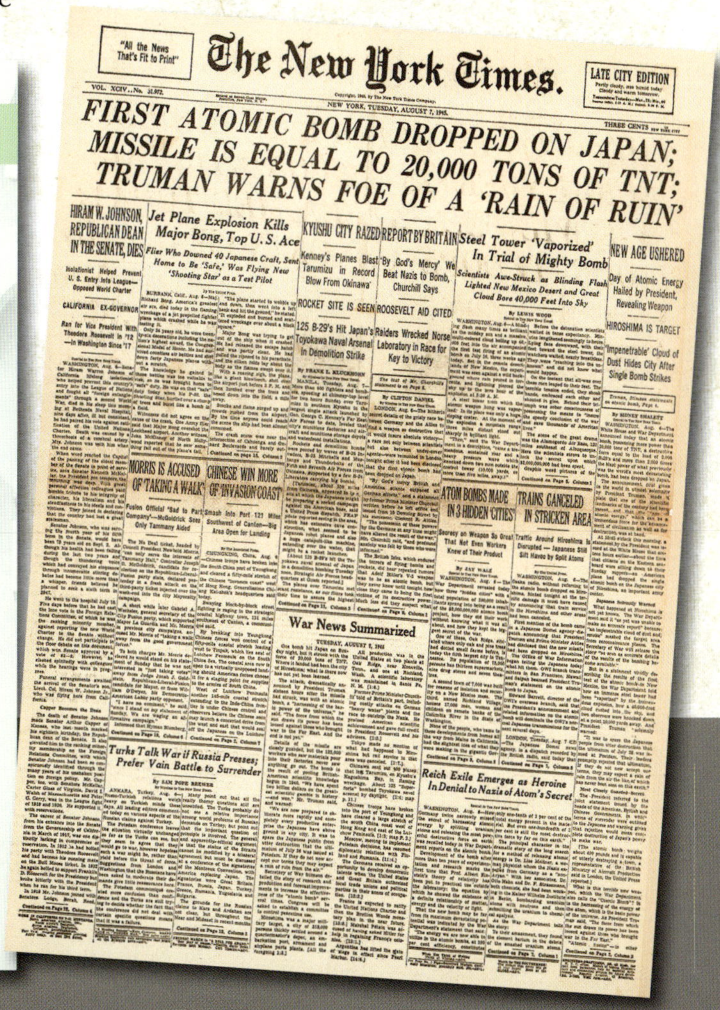
"All the News That's Fit to Print"
The New York Times.
LATE CITY EDITION
NEW YORK, TUESDAY, AUGUST 7, 1945.
THREE CENTS
FIRST ATOMIC BOMB DROPPED ON JAPAN; MISSILE IS EQUAL TO 20,000 TONS OF TNT; TRUMAN WARNS FOE OF A 'RAIN OF RUIN'
HIRAM W. JOHNSON, REPUBLICAN DEAN IN THE SENATE, DIES
Jet Plane Explosion Kills Major Bong, Top U.S. Ace
KYUSHU CITY RAZED
REPORT BY BRITAIN
Steel Tower 'Vaporized' In Trial of Mighty Bomb
NEW AGE USHERED
ROCKET SITE IS SEEN
ROOSEVELT AID CITED
HIROSHIMA IS TARGET
MORRIS IS ACCUSED OF 'TAKING A WALK'
CHINESE WIN MORE OF 'INVASION COAST'
ATOM BOMBS MADE IN 3 HIDDEN 'CITIES'
TRAINS CANCELED IN STRICKEN AREA
War News Summarized
Turks Talk War if Russia Presses; Prefer Vain Battle to Surrender
Reich Exile Emerges as Heroine In Denial to Nazis of Atom's Secret

PERSPECTIVES

In 1945, a group of scientists at the University of Chicago who had helped develop nuclear energy technology became concerned about the possible use of nuclear bombs. In 1947, they introduced the "Doomsday Clock" to indicate the sense of urgency to the global threat of nuclear war. The time was set to seven minutes to midnight. The closest the clock has been to midnight was in 1953, when both the United States and the U.S.S.R. tested thermonuclear weapons. It showed 2 minutes to 12. Currently the clock is set at 2 $^1/_2$ minutes to 12.

▲ **Based on the 1958 novel *Red Alert* by Peter George, the 1964 movie *Dr. Strangelove* is about the fear of nuclear war between the United States and the U.S.S.R.**

SECONDARY SOURCES

Secondary sources are created by people who do not have firsthand experience of a specific event. They are created at a later date and are an interpretation of the period based on what the creator has learned by analyzing other source materials. Like primary sources, secondary sources can be written or visual. Examples of secondary sources include movies, paintings, drawings, charts, graphs, books, and biographies. Often, people who create secondary sources collect, analyze, and organize primary source materials into usable information. Secondary sources are a great way to quickly get a glimpse into the past.

There are many Hollywood movies based on the Arms Race and the fears of society at the time. *On the Beach*, released in 1959, explored what life would be like if all of Earth except Australia was destroyed by a nuclear bomb. Stanley Kubrick's 1964 movie *Dr. Strangelove* told the story of a U.S. military man who decides to bomb the Soviet Union.

Other secondary sources include popular fiction books, such as *The Butter Battle Book* by Dr. Seuss, and comic books featuring characters such as Iron

"I have to bring to your notice a terrifying reality: with the development of nuclear weapons Man has acquired, for the first time in history, the technical means to destroy the whole of civilization in a single act."

Polish physicist Joseph Rotblat, accepting the Nobel Peace Prize in 1995

Man. These reflected the concerns of society around the time of the Arms Race. The movie *Tinker Tailor Soldier Spy* was based on a book by John le Carré. It tells the story of a British intelligence agent on the hunt for a Soviet spy. In 1990, Tom Clancy's book *The Hunt for Red October* was made into a major movie starring Sean Connery and Alec Baldwin. It followed the story of CIA agent Jack Ryan as he tried to figure out why a Russian submarine captain decided to disobey orders and head into U.S. waters.

▲ **Soviet nuclear physicist Igor Kurchatov, who created the Soviet atomic bomb, was featured on a U.S.S.R. stamp in 1963.**

◀ ***Barefoot Gen: A Cartoon Story of Hiroshima*, Vol. 1, released in 2004, is a firsthand account of what it was like to survive Hiroshima and cope with its impact.**

ANALYZE THIS

Why is it important to hear the story of Hiroshima through the eyes of a survivor? What can we learn by reading about this person's point of view?

INTERPRETATION

"Nuclear weapons are intrinsically neither moral nor immoral, though they are more prone to immoral use than most weapons."

Herman Kahn, U.S. military strategist, 1984

Historians are like detectives. They look to many different types of source materials to find clues about past events. They analyze and interpret each source to see if it is valid, useful, and **accurate**. Some sources may support or contradict the historian's own ideas about the past. Other sources may contradict one another or contain false information. It is important for historians to be open-minded to different viewpoints to ensure they get a **balanced** view of history. They need to decide which sources are the most trustworthy. Sometimes, historians even decide their own conclusions about the past are incorrect.

How do historians determine if a source is **credible**? They can look at the **credentials** of the person or organization that created it. They can also look at when the source was created or published and who published it. They decide whether it is a primary or secondary source. They question the creator's point of view and if it shapes the information provided in the source. If it tries to change a person's perspective of history, the source is biased.

What bias might people have when looking at evidence of the Arms Race? At the time, the Soviet Union wanted to spread communism across the world. Fears of communism were strong in the United States and Canada. Think about the Soviet perspective versus the North American perspective and how their biases may have impacted source materials created during this period.

PERSPECTIVES

Look at this photograph of a nuclear test. What is your overall impression? What do you see? List three things you might infer about this photograph based on your observations.

◀ On May 25, 1953, the U.S. military conducted the Upshot–Knothole test in Nevada, the first-ever test of a nuclear artillery shell.

ANALYZING BIAS

When a source is biased, it shows a clear preference in favor of or against an idea, person, place, event, or object. It is influenced by the creator's personal beliefs or opinions or those of society in general. Some people intentionally include bias in their sources. Others don't mean to include it. For example, imagine you have to write a report about your favorite sports team or TV program. Now think how hard it will be to write a critical, balanced, and unbiased report if your team lost its last game badly or all your friends don't like the TV program.

For a source to be credible, it should be based on fact and be **impartial**, so people can form their own opinions based on the information provided. To find out if a source is biased, historians look to see if the author has:

- Omitted or stretched facts
- Made positive or negative word choices
- Included additional, unnecessary details
- Included extreme language
- Presented political views
- Misquoted a source or failed to cite sources

Historians need to consider how certain factors, such as religion, money, and politics, can influence a person's perspective. To ensure they have a broad

PERSPECTIVES

What does this cartoon tell you about the artist's view of world peace? Who is the intended audience? How do you think it made people feel?

▶ In 1948 Rube Goldberg won the Pulitzer Prize for his political cartoon about the atomic bomb called *Peace Today*.

view of history that takes into account many points of view, historians look for a variety of primary sources created by different people. When interpreting a source, historians ask certain questions to determine if it is biased:

- Who created the source? What is this person's education or experience? Were they paid to create it?
- Why was the source created? What purpose does it serve?
- Does the source present more than one point of view?
- When was the source created? How much time passed between the period being studied and the source being made?
- Who was the source created for? Did the target audience have an impact on how the information is presented?

When reading source material, historians think about the **context**, or circumstances, at that time. What were the common beliefs and customs? What other things were happening in the world? The Arms Race happened when there was immense competition between the U.S.S.R. and the United States. This had a major impact on the bias of Arms Race material produced by all countries involved, which included Canada, Great Britain, France, and China.

◀ In 1962 Ben Sahn created an anti-nuclear poster for a New York-based group called the National Committee for a SANE Nuclear Policy. It related to hydrogen bombs **(see page 27).**

"Communism counts its opportunities in terms of decades—not of weeks. Its means of aggression consist not only of nuclear weapons and missiles with enormous boosters, and not only of spies, agents and terrorists, but of great masses of men and women, deluded by a common ideology which inspires them with a false hope."

U.S. politician Robert Kennedy, 1962

THE STORY UNCOVERED

THE NUCLEAR ARMS RACE

"When I was in the White House, I was confronted with the challenge of the Cold War. Both the Soviet Union and I had 30,000 nuclear weapons that could destroy the entire earth and I had to maintain the peace."

Jimmy Carter, Jr., U.S. president 1977–1981

The discovery of nuclear fission in 1938 paved the way for the development of nuclear arms. When German scientists Otto Hahn, Lise Meitner, and Otto Frisch discovered how to split uranium atoms to create massive amounts of energy, they changed the world forever. Within a year, World War II had started and scientists across the globe were thinking how nuclear fission could be used to build atomic weapons. Concerned about the potential dangers of atomic energy in the hands of the **Axis Powers**, scientists Albert Einstein and Enrico Fermi, who had fled **fascist** Germany and Italy respectively, each issued a warning to President Franklin D. Roosevelt in 1939. At their urging, Roosevelt eventually agreed to provide $6,000 to fund a project to harness the power of nuclear fission.

Code-named the Manhattan Project, U.S. scientists started work on the first atomic bomb in December 1941. Fermi took an active role in the highly secretive project. At first, research was restricted to just a few key universities across the country. However, that all changed when Fermi and a team of scientists produced the first controlled chain reaction using nuclear fission on December 2, 1942, at the University of Chicago. After that, the Manhattan Project grew massively. By 1943, Canada and Great Britain had partnered on the project, sending several scientists to the United States to help with the effort.

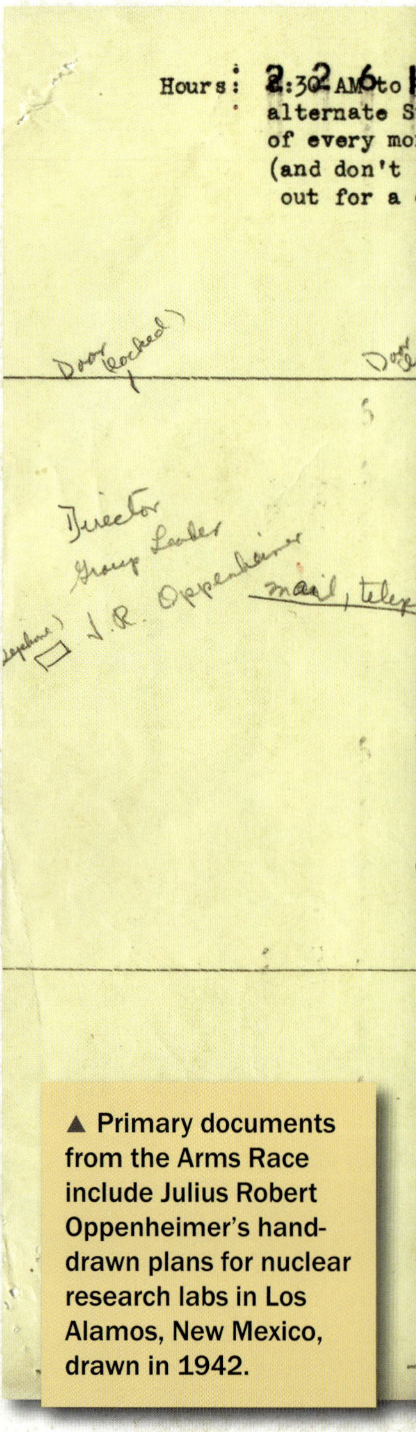

▲ Primary documents from the Arms Race include Julius Robert Oppenheimer's hand-drawn plans for nuclear research labs in Los Alamos, New Mexico, drawn in 1942.

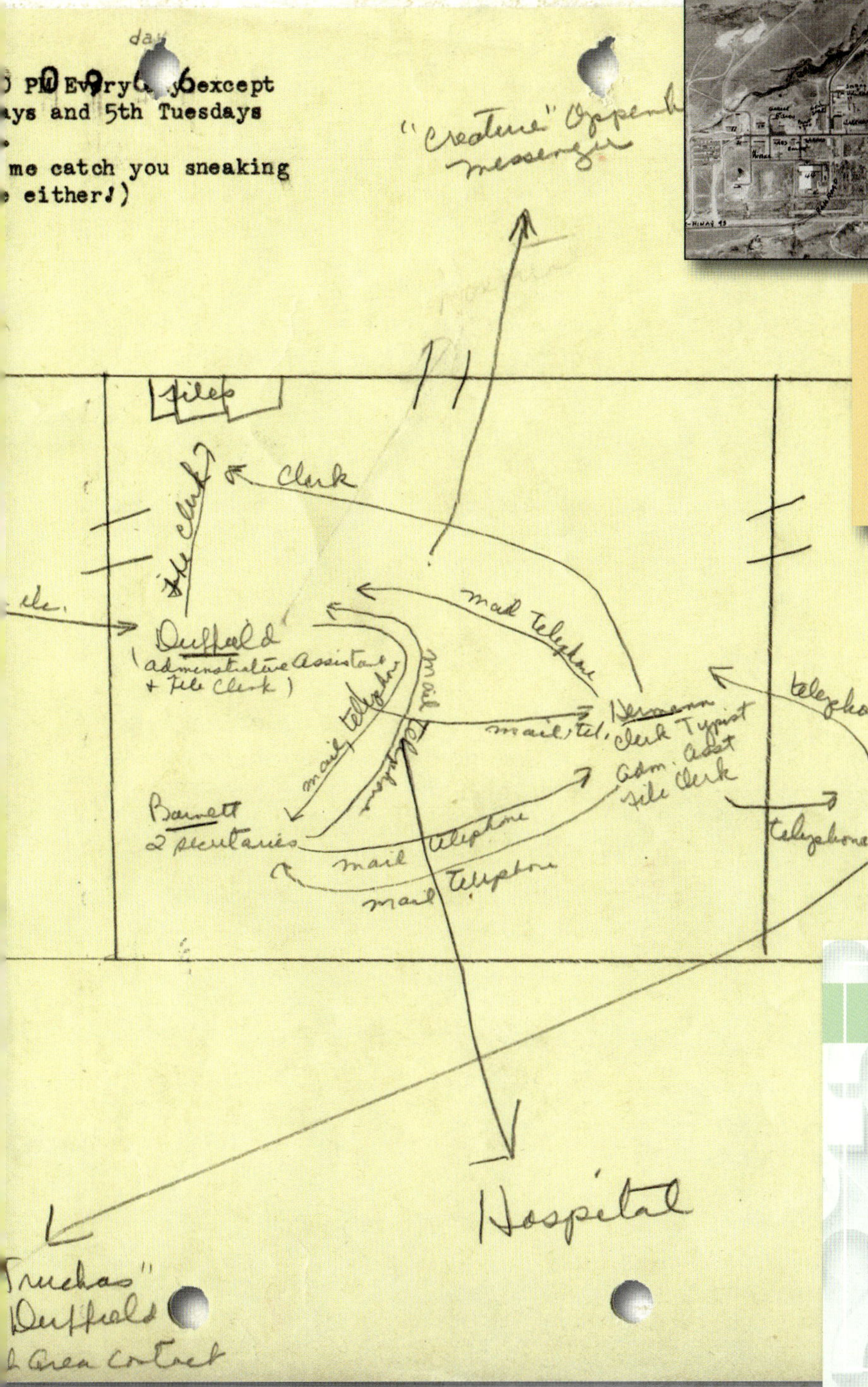

▲ An aerial photo taken in 1964 shows the Dow Chemical Company's Rocky Flats nuclear plant in Los Alamos, New Mexico.

PERSPECTIVES

What does this drawing tell you about the Los Alamos labs? What types of buildings and features did Oppenheimer include in the plans? What do the typed words on top say? What do you think they mean?

BOMBS AWAY

Enrico Fermi's work spurred on the Manhattan Project. The U.S. government poured about $2 billion into the project, which at its height employed about 130,000 people at nearly 40 facilities. In 1943, Julius Robert Oppenheimer, an accomplished nuclear scientist, was placed in charge of the main facility in Los Alamos, New Mexico. Known as the "father of the atomic bomb," Oppenheimer supervised the team that put together the first nuclear weapon. Finally, the Americans were ready to test their invention. In the early hours of the morning of July 16, 1945, the bomb was **detonated** at a military test facility in Alamogordo, New Mexico. Known as the Trinity Test, its earth-shattering impact was felt as far as 50 miles (80 km) away. Hours later, the armed forces released a carefully crafted cover story explaining away the blinding light and 40,000-foot (12,192 m) high mushroom cloud that accompanied the explosion.

Because of its top-secret nature, the **Allies** worked hard to ensure the Axis Powers had no idea about the Manhattan Project. Knowledge of the project was so restricted that even Harry S. Truman, who was vice-president at the time, did not learn about it until after he became president in April 1945. While the Soviets and the Americans were on the same side during World War II, there was distrust between them due to their radically different political views. Even though the nuclear bomb was being developed with a mutual interest in mind—defeating the Axis Powers—the Americans did not tell the Soviets about the Manhattan Project.

▼ On July 14, 1945, workers prepared the first atomic device for the Trinity Test that would take place two days later at the Alamogordo Bombing and Gunnery Range, now part of the U.S. Army's White Sands Missile Range in the Jornada del Muerto Valley, New Mexico.

◀ **Klaus Fuchs was a British scientist who worked on the Manhattan Project and passed project details to Soviet spies.**

DAILY NEWS NEW YORK'S PICTURE NEWSPAPER 3¢

NAL

No. 20

New York 17, Tuesday, July 18, 1950

64 Pages

GIs HOLD REDS NEAR TAEJON

Story on Page 3

(NEWS foto by Art Whittaker)

Another Broken Link in Red Spy Chain. Described by FBI Chief J. Edgar Hoover as "another important link in the Soviet espionage apparatus," Julius Rosenberg (center, hatless), 32-year-old New York-born engineer, is taken by FBI agents into Federal Building, Foley Square, last night. He was arrested in Knickerbocker Village apartment as one of Klaus Fuchs-Gold spy ring which passed atom secrets to Russia. —Story on page 2

▲ On July 18, 1950, the cover of the *New York Daily News* showed Julius Rosenberg (center), a 32-year-old New York engineer, being taken into custody by FBI agents for his role in passing nuclear secrets to Soviet spies.

Indeed, the Soviets did not officially find out about it until days after the first test bomb was exploded. Unofficially, however, they had known about it for some time, thanks to a Soviet spy ring that penetrated the project as early as 1941. With so many people at work on the project, it was nearly impossible to keep people from talking about it.

By this time, the war in Europe was over. However, it was still raging in the Pacific. Despite warnings that the use of an atomic bomb would result in tens of thousands of deaths, President Harry S. Truman decided it was necessary to use the nation's new weapons technology to save American lives and end the war. On August 6, 1945, a U.S. bomber dropped an atomic bomb on Hiroshima, Japan. Three days later, a second atomic bomb was dropped on Nagasaki.

PERSPECTIVES

What type of source material is this? What are the people in this picture doing? Who do you think they are? What do the looks on their faces tell you about how they were feeling? What do the headline and caption heading tell you about what is happening here?

"The superpowers often behave like two heavily armed blind men feeling their way around a room, each believing himself in mortal peril from the other, whom he assumes to have perfect vision."

U.S. secretary of state Henry Kissinger, 1999

THE COMPETITION INCREASES

Following the nuclear bombings in Japan, many scientists who had worked on the Manhattan Project created the Federation of Atomic Scientists (FAS). Believing they should use their knowledge of nuclear energy to benefit society, the FAS wanted to encourage **civilian** control over atomic research, reduce the level of secrecy surrounding nuclear energy projects, and educate the public about the potentially devastating effects of nuclear energy. A few months later, the United Nations formed the Atomic Energy Commission (UNAEC). Made up of six permanent members—the United States, Great Britain, France, the Soviet Union, China, and Canada—as well as six rotating members, the committee acted as an international advisor on nuclear energy.

In March 1946 a U.S. policy committee

PERSPECTIVES

The Marshall Plan was devised by and named for U.S. secretary of state George C. Marshall. It aimed to reduce the influence of communist parties within Western Europe. Who do you think created this picture? What was this person's point of view? How does it make you feel? How do you think it made people feel at the time?

▶ The Marshall Plan provided funds to help rebuild Western Europe after World War II. This West German poster from the late 1940s states that the "Marshall Plan helps Europe."

issued the Acheson–Lilienthal Report recognizing the need for an international organization to regulate the development of nuclear weapons and monitor atomic energy research. The report recommended that UNAEC form a committee to fulfill this role. However, the U.S. government rejected the recommendation since it would require the country to hand over **classified** atomic research. Following the discovery of Soviet spies in the United States, the government feared the Soviets would use U.S. research against Americans.

A few months later, the U.S. diplomat Bernard Baruch suggested that UNAEC regulate all international nuclear energy research and prohibit possession of atomic weapons. The committee would have the right to perform inspections of nuclear facilities to ensure compliance with the plan. The U.S.S.R. rejected this idea because it favored the United States.

KEEPING ATOMIC ENERGY UNDER CONTROL

With no agreement, the United States forged ahead with its own nuclear policy. President Truman signed the Atomic Energy Act into law on August 1, 1946, setting up the Atomic Energy Commission (AEC). The AEC took over control of all atomic research and development projects in the United States.

The Canadian government followed suit with the Atomic Energy Control Act on October 12. Under the act, the Atomic Energy Control Board (AECB) would supervise Canada's involvement in nuclear energy projects. Both nations wanted to ensure any future work on atomic energy would improve public welfare and promote world peace. Initiatives included **biomedical** applications and nuclear power plants.

▲ **Copies of the first Soviet atomic bomb RDS-1 (bottom of the photo)—nicknamed by the United States as "Joe-1" after the Soviet premier Joseph Stalin—and its first hydrogen bomb, RDS-6 (center), in a Russian museum.**

"Ours is a world of nuclear giants and ethical infants. We know more about war than we know about peace, more about killing than we know about living. The way to win an atomic war is to make certain it never starts. And the way to make sure it never starts is to abolish the dangerous costly nuclear stockpiles which imprison mankind."

American general Omar Bradley, speaking on Armistice Day, 1948

RAISING THE STAKES

For a while, nuclear weapons projects took a backseat to atomic energy research. That ended when President Truman unveiled the Truman Doctrine in 1947. In an effort to contain communism, Truman pledged support for countries that were under threat of communist takeover, in particular Greece and Turkey. The doctrine bolstered the belief that the United States needed to prepare for war with the U.S.S.R.

While the Americans were building their **arsenal** of atomic weapons, the Soviets were working hard on nuclear technology of their own. In 1949 they tested their first atomic bomb, known as "First Lightning." The U.S.S.R. was only the second nation to test a nuclear weapon, and it took the world by surprise. The nuclear Arms Race had officially begun.

In October 1952, Great Britain joined the race, testing its first atomic weapon off the coast of Australia. By this time, the United States and the U.S.S.R. had moved on to newer technologies. Both nations began to invest

ANALYZE THIS

When you see an image of a mushroom cloud, what thoughts go through your mind and why? Do you think scientists of the time knew about **radioactive fallout** from the explosions? If they did, why might they not have told the general public?

FINAL

DAILY NEW

NEW YORK'S PICTURE NEWSPAPER

BRITISH SET OFF FIRST A-BOMB

Blast Off Australia Is 'Different'

▼ **Headlines in the *New York Daily News* told of the first British atomic bomb test, which took place on October 3, 1952.**

heavily in researching and developing the hydrogen bomb. American scientists became particularly interested in Edward Teller's work on **nuclear fusion** to create a hydrogen-, or H-, bomb that was 1,000 times more powerful than an atomic bomb.

Born in Budapest, Hungary, in 1908, Teller was a respected theoretical physicist who had worked with Oppenheimer and Fermi on the Manhattan Project. Teller's growing interest in developing a super bomb caused tension among the other scientists. Eventually, Teller convinced President Truman to fund his research into the H-bomb. Now that the Soviets had atomic weapons of their own, Teller believed the United States needed more powerful means of protecting itself. Oppenheimer spoke out against Teller, vocalizing concerns over fusion weapons and the destruction they could bring the human race. Fermi also recommended against building a super bomb. Truman ordered its development anyway.

◀ A mushroom cloud of smoke and debris from the first successful hydrogen bomb test (see page 28). Teller helped develop the bomb but was not involved in its use.

EVIDENCE RECORD CARD

Image of the "Ivy Mike" explosion
LEVEL Primary source
MATERIAL Color photograph
LOCATION Elugelab, Marshall Islands, Pacific Ocean
DATE November 1, 1952
SOURCE Getty Images

"A nuclear war cannot be won and must never be fought. The only value in our two nations possessing nuclear weapons is to make sure they will never be used. But then would it not be better to do away with them entirely."

U.S. President Ronald Reagan in his 1984 State of the Union Address

NUCLEAR FALLOUT

Less than a month after the British exploded their first nuclear weapon, the Americans put Teller's technology to the test. On November 1, 1952, they detonated the world's first hydrogen bomb on Enewetak, an uninhabited atoll in the Marshall Islands. The massive 20-foot (6 m) high, 82-ton (74 metric ton) device resulted in an explosion 700 times more massive than the atomic bomb dropped on Hiroshima seven years earlier. Known as "Ivy Mike," the bomb created an enormous cloud that rose more than 30 miles (48 km) into the sky and killed all wildlife and vegetation on the atoll and nearby islands. Nothing was left of Enewetak but a crater.

Less than a year later, Soviet premier Georgy Malenkov revealed that the Soviets had developed their own H-bomb technology. It was based on information stolen from the Americans by Klaus Fuchs, a British scientist who had worked on the Manhattan Project. Fuchs passed information to American chemist Harry Gold, who was a Soviet spy. On August 12, 1953, the U.S.S.R. tested its first **thermonuclear** device. Unlike "Ivy Mike," it was small enough to be dropped from a plane, making it ready to use in combat missions. Though not a true hydrogen bomb, it showed the Soviets were still major players in the Arms Race.

A few months later, on March 1, 1954, Castle Bravo was exploded on Bikini Atoll in the Marshall Islands. At 15 megatons of TNT, it was the most powerful nuclear device detonated by the United States. With more than double the expected output, the Americans severely underestimated the impact of the bomb. Radioactive **contamination** spread to several islands, causing many

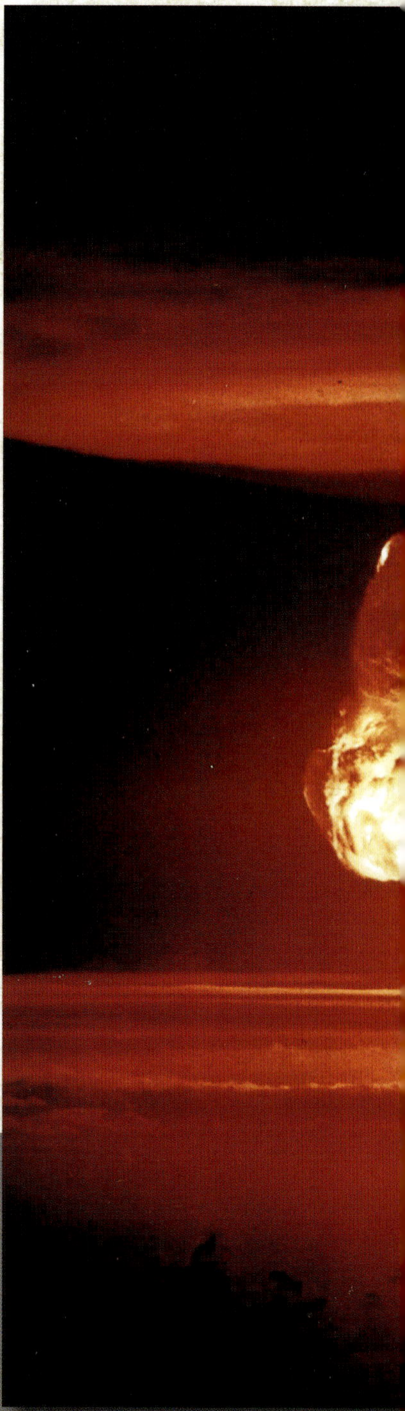

"The Bulletin's clock is not a gauge to register the ups and downs of the international power struggle; it is intended to reflect basic changes in the level of continuous danger in which mankind lives in the nuclear age."

Eugene Rabinowitch, *Bulletin of Atomic Scientists*, creator of the Doomsday Clock (see page 13.)

▼ **The United States carried out 67 nuclear weapons tests in the Pacific Ocean from 1946 to 1958, including Castle Bravo on Bikini Atoll in March 1954.**

people to become ill and killing a man aboard a Japanese fishing boat about 80 miles (129 km) from the test site. Some people thought the powder that fell from the sky was snow. They played in it, not realizing it was deadly.

PERSPECTIVES

The U.S. government recommended people build fallout shelters in their basements or underground in their backyards. Look at this photo taken inside a fallout shelter. Who are the people in the photo? What are they doing? What objects are inside the shelter?

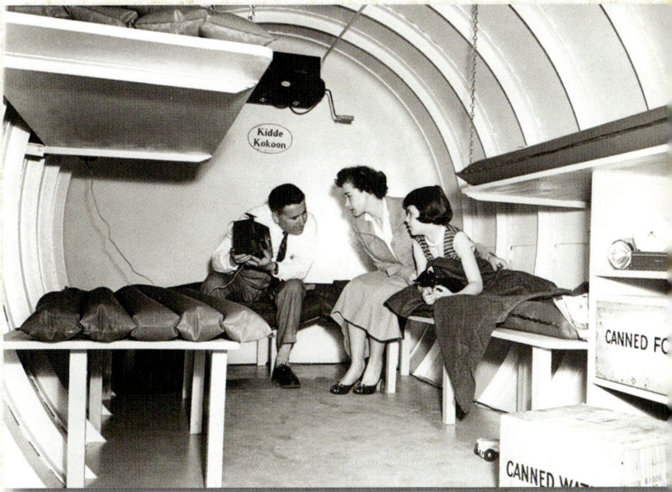

▲ **Nuclear fallout shelters meant to safeguard people from nuclear attacks and radiation were popular in the 1950s.**

ANALYZE THIS

The Arms Race happened before the Internet existed. How do you think U.S. and Soviet spies got their information? How might spies have been watched and detected? What do you think U.S. citizens felt about Soviet spying?

PLEAS FOR PEACE

Traces of the fallout from the Castle Bravo test were found up to 7,000 miles (11,265 km) away in Japan, Australia, and Europe. About 665 people in the Marshall Islands were exposed to the radiation, resulting in birth defects and other health issues. Residents were not **evacuated** for days after the testing. They were allowed to return a few years later but were forced to leave again when the islands were found to be unsafe. People called for **atmospheric** testing of nuclear bombs to be banned.

Following the devastating Castle Bravo testing, 11 scientists, including 10 Nobel Laureates, put forward the Russell–Einstein Manifesto on July 9, 1955. In it, they urged world leaders to end nuclear arms testing and development. Albert Einstein, whose theory and equation $E = mc^2$ gave birth to the atomic bomb, added his name to the statement only nine days before his death. But the Arms Race continued. On November 22, 1955, the Soviets tested their first true hydrogen bomb.

The introduction of **intercontinental ballistic missiles** (ICBMs) in the 1950s made it possible to launch missiles

▼ A Soviet image of the remains of the U-2 spy plane flown by U.S. pilot Francis Gary Powers, which was shot down on May 1, 1960, over Soviet airspace. Powers was kept prisoner for two years before being swapped for a Soviet spy.

at targets thousands of miles away. In fact, the Soviets used an ICBM to launch the world's first artificial **satellite**, *Sputnik 1*, into space in 1957. In 1958, United Nations Secretary-General Dag Hammarskjöld received a petition signed by about 10,000 scientists calling for world leaders to put an end to the production of nuclear weapons. That same year, the United States, the Soviet Union, and Great Britain agreed to stop nuclear testing as part of the Partial Test Ban Treaty.

▼ **Albert Einstein on a 1950 cover of a German satirical magazine *Der Simpl*. He was opposed to using nuclear bombs.**

TALKS BREAK DOWN

Negotiations between the superpowers continued over the next few years. Both the United States and Great Britain wanted onsite inspections to ensure the Soviets were abiding by the terms of the test ban agreement. However, the U.S.S.R. was opposed to the idea, believing it was just a way for other countries to spy on it. Talks broke down completely when the Soviets shot down a U.S. spy plane over Russia in 1960.

> *"We have to learn to think in a new way. We have to learn to ask ourselves, not what steps can be taken to give military victory to whatever group we prefer, for there no longer are such steps; the question we have to ask ourselves is: what steps can be taken to prevent a military contest of which the issue must be disastrous to all parties?"*
>
> Excerpt from the Russell-Einstein Manifesto

THE CUBAN MISSILE CRISIS

While the United States and the U.S.S.R. were competing with each other, other countries had built their own nuclear weapons. By 1960, Great Britain had been investing deeply in atomic research for nearly two decades and had tested atomic bombs. France tested its first nuclear weapon in 1960, and China was building its first nuclear bomb.

Throughout the 1950s, both the United States and the U.S.S.R. stockpiled enough arms to cause mass destruction. Neither one attacked the other because they knew it would lead to **retaliation**. However, the Cuban Missile Crisis proved how ready both powers were to head into battle.

In 1961 U.S. President John Kennedy had ordered an invasion of Cuba by CIA-backed exiles to force out Fidel Castro's communist regime. The Bay of Pigs invasion lasted less than 24 hours. Castro's army severely outnumbered the invaders, resulting in defeat for the Americans. Castro wanted to prevent a similar invasion in the future. A partnership with the Soviet Union was the perfect solution. In July 1962 he reached agreement with Soviet premier

ANALYZE THIS

Do you think President Kennedy and Nikita Khrushchev were right in their attitudes and decisions? Why or why not? What do you think would have happened if the U.S. had invaded Cuba?

▶ **During the Cuban Missile Crisis in 1962, U.S. Navy destroyer DD-878 intercepted the missile-bearing Soviet ship *Potzunov*. The crisis also involved U.S. missile sites in Turkey, which were later removed.**

Nikita Khrushchev to place Soviet missiles in Cuba. When the U.S. government learned about the Soviet missile sites being built in Cuba, it quickly responded.

On October 22, President Kennedy went on live U.S. television to announce plans for a naval blockade around Cuba. The United States was willing to take all necessary measures to protect itself from the Soviet threat. People worldwide braced themselves for a nuclear war. After 13 days, the standoff came to an end when Khrushchev agreed to remove Soviet missiles from Cuba if Kennedy promised not to invade it. Months later, a nuclear test ban treaty was signed.

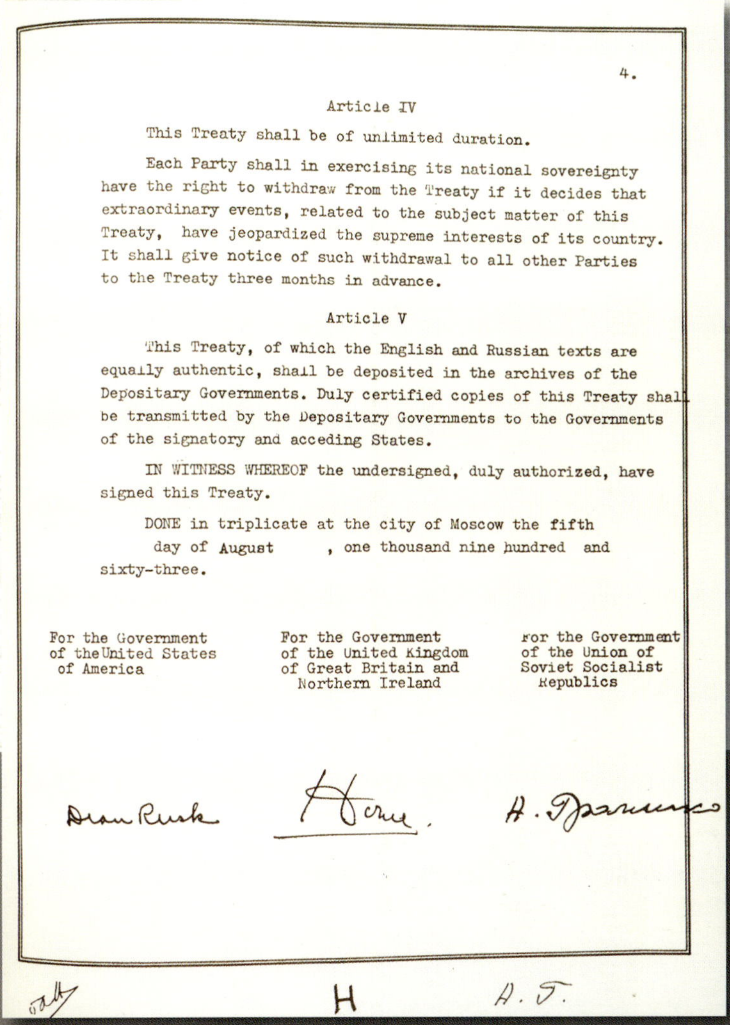

4.

Article IV

This Treaty shall be of unlimited duration.

Each Party shall in exercising its national sovereignty have the right to withdraw from the Treaty if it decides that extraordinary events, related to the subject matter of this Treaty, have jeopardized the supreme interests of its country. It shall give notice of such withdrawal to all other Parties to the Treaty three months in advance.

Article V

This Treaty, of which the English and Russian texts are equally authentic, shall be deposited in the archives of the Depositary Governments. Duly certified copies of this Treaty shall be transmitted by the Depositary Governments to the Governments of the signatory and acceding States.

IN WITNESS WHEREOF the undersigned, duly authorized, have signed this Treaty.

DONE in triplicate at the city of Moscow the fifth day of August, one thousand nine hundred and sixty-three.

For the Government of the United States of America	For the Government of the United Kingdom of Great Britain and Northern Ireland	For the Government of the Union of Soviet Socialist Republics
Dean Rusk	Home	А. Громыко

On August 5, 1963, U.S. secretary of state Dean Rusk, foreign secretary of Great Britain Lord Home, and Soviet foreign minister Andrei Gromyko signed the Limited Nuclear Test Ban Treaty, restricting nuclear weapons testing.

EVIDENCE RECORD CARD

Signed image of the Limited Nuclear Test Ban Treaty

LEVEL Primary source
MATERIAL Document
LOCATION Moscow, U.S.S.R.
DATE August 5, 1963
SOURCE Getty Images

"If you go on with this nuclear arms race, all you are going to do is make the rubble bounce."

British prime minister Winston Churchill, 1952

SLOW IT DOWN

"The peoples of this world must unite or they will perish."

Julius Robert Oppenheimer, from his farewell speech on his last working day at Los Alamos, October 16, 1945

Something had to be done to ease the tension between the United States and the Soviet Union following the Cuban Missile Crisis. The Limited Test Ban Treaty came into effect on August 5, 1963. Signed originally by the U.S., Soviet, and British governments, it banned all atmospheric, space, and underwater nuclear testing. Although China and France refused to sign, it was still a major step in the right direction. With the costs of developing more powerful arms mounting, the treaty was a welcome relief to slow the pace of the Arms Race.

Talks to further prevent the spread of nuclear weapons technology continued, and in 1968, the Non-Proliferation Treaty was signed. Countries that signed agreed not to develop or acquire nuclear arms from other nations and to promote the use of nuclear energy for peaceful projects.

At the start of the Arms Race, the U.S. and Soviet governments were eager to develop more powerful atomic weapons. But that changed in the 1960s and 1970s when the cost of producing new weapons began to weigh down the economies of both nations. People grew more aware of the power behind atomic weapons and became more wary of them. A wave of anti-nuclear protests spread and groups such as the Committee for a Sane Nuclear Policy (started in 1957) and Women Strike for Peace (established in 1961) became active. In addition, many of the scientists who helped design the first atomic bombs now **campaigned** against them. Support for the development of nuclear arms was waning.

▶ This frame house was destroyed by a nuclear blast on March 17, 1953 at the Nevada test site.

ANALYZE THIS

Make a list of the people and objects you see in this picture. What concept or idea do you think the photographer is trying to get across? Was the photographer trying to make people feel a certain way?

◀ Workers hold up a picture showing what the building behind them looked like before nuclear test Operation CUE took place on May 5, 1955, and destroyed most of the buildings in Survival Town, Nevada.

DIFFERENT VIEWS

STAR WARS

The Strategic Arms Limitation Talks (SALT) between the United States and the U.S.S.R. began in 1969, resulting in several treaties. Henry Kissinger, head of the U.S. National Security Council, helped negotiate the first treaty in 1972. SALT I put a freeze on new ICBMs and submarine-launched ballistic missiles (SLBMs) for five years. Loopholes led to the United States and the U.S.S.R. adding thousands of new warheads to their collections and replacing old weapons with more powerful ones. SALT II, which came into effect in 1979, aimed to place more limitations on nuclear weapons. However, when the Soviets invaded Afghanistan in 1980, the Americans retaliated by refusing to agree to the treaty and once again increasing their spending on nuclear arms.

During his presidential campaign against President Jimmy Carter in 1980, Ronald Reagan made it clear that he felt SALT II was flawed. He won the election, and on March 23, 1983, President Reagan announced plans to implement the Strategic Defense Initiative (SDI). This anti-ballistic missile program was aimed at preventing nuclear attacks from afar. Complete with space-based lasers and other futuristic ideas, SDI seemed like

ANALYZE THIS

What effects, if any, do you think the end of the Cold War, the Star Wars program, and the fall of the Berlin Wall had on other countries of the world? Are these effects in evidence today? Do you think they are good or bad effects?

"The atom bomb fueled the entire world that came after it. It showed that indiscriminate killing and indiscriminate homicide on a mass level was possible ..."

American singer-songwriter Bob Dylan, interviewed in *Rolling Stone*, May 3, 2007

▲ Soviet general secretary Mikhail Gorbachev and U.S. President Ronald Reagan signed the Intermediate-Range Nuclear Forces Treaty in the East Room at the White House in 1987.

something out of a science-fiction movie. Nicknamed "Star Wars," the initiative sparked renewed tension with the Soviet Union for stepping outside the **sanctions** of the SALT agreement.

Over time, President Reagan grew concerned over possible Soviet retaliation and began to build a new and friendlier relationship with the new Soviet premier Mikhail Gorbachev instead. By 1987, the two leaders were in talks to forge a new agreement. Signed on June 1, 1988, the Intermediate-Range Nuclear Forces (INF) Treaty called for both countries to destroy certain types of weapons from their arsenals. The groundbreaking agreement also included measures for verification and onsite inspections.

It was about this time that many of the 15 **republics** making up the U.S.S.R. began to revolt against their communist governments. By 1991, each one had declared its independence from the Soviet Union. Gorbachev resigned on December 25, and the U.S.S.R. was dissolved. The Cold War had come to an end.

PERSPECTIVES

The Berlin Wall started to be taken apart on November 9, 1989, and people could cross freely from East to West Berlin. Look at this photo of East German border guards removing parts of the wall. Do you think the guards were pleased, concerned, or fearful about the likely outcome? Why, or why not?

◀ As the U.S.S.R. began to crumble, so, too, did the Berlin Wall that had divided communist East and capitalist West Berlin since 1961. The wall eventually fell in November 1989, leading to the reunification of Berlin and of Germany.

MODERN EXAMPLES

HISTORY REPEATED

"We can say with certainty—we are stronger now than any potential aggressor. Anyone."

Russian President Vladimir Putin, 2016

Although the Cold War between the United States and the U.S.S.R. ended in the 1990s when both countries agreed to nuclear controls, tensions have been on the rise again in recent years. In December 2016 U.S. President-elect Donald Trump raised the world's attention when he tweeted: "The United States must greatly strengthen and expand its nuclear capability until such time as the world comes to its senses regarding nukes."

Trump later confirmed his stance that the United States would not sit by idly while other countries built up their arms. President Vladimir Putin of Russia said that he was not surprised by Trump's statements. After taking office as president, Trump continued to assert that he would support a renewed Arms Race.

In the last 20 years or so, other nations around the world have developed nuclear weapons as a way to assert their power and deter potential enemy threats. Only five countries are legally allowed to have nuclear weapons—the United States, Great Britain, Russia, France, and China. To date, nine countries have access to nuclear arms, including Pakistan, India, Israel, and North Korea. Most only have a few dozen to a few hundred nuclear weapons in their arsenal. The United States and Russia maintain about 90 percent of the global supply, with more than 7,000 each. Five European nations have allowed the United States to place nuclear weapons on their soil, and about 24 other nations rely on U.S. nuclear arms for security.

▼ On January 6, 2016, a newspaper in Tokyo, Japan, had a photo of North Korean leader Kim Jong-Un announcing his country had performed its first hydrogen bomb test.

PERSPECTIVES

Why do you think people in Japan would want to know about hydrogen bomb tests in North Korea? Why do you think the headline is so large? How might the newspaper article have made readers feel? What might North Korean newspapers have said?

MODERN EXAMPLES

MODERN-DAY ARMS RACES

In 1947, the neighboring Asian countries of India and Pakistan gained indepedence from Great Britain. It immediately sparked a two-year war over control of Kashmir, a territory that spans the countries. War erupted again in 1965. On May 18, 1974, India tested its first atomic bomb. Testing resumed on May 11, 1998, when India detonated three massive nuclear weapons. In response, Pakistan showed that it, too, had nuclear capabilities, performing several nuclear tests on May 28, 1998. A third India–Pakistan war followed in 1999 and possession of Kashmir is still an unresolved issue.

Also in Asia, in 1950 the Korean War started. A Soviet-backed North Korean army invaded South Korea. The United States supported South Korea to stop the spread of communism, and considered use of a nuclear bomb to end the war. As a result, North Korea started to develop nuclear weapons technology. Although the Korean War ended in 1953, this arms race continued.

In 2001, U.S. President George W. Bush called Iran, Iraq, and North Korea an "axis of evil" that posed a major threat to the United States. Bush suggested the three nations were stockpiling weapons of mass destruction, such as nuclear arms, and providing support to terrorist groups. Bush turned out to be wrong about Iraq, and Iran has since halted its nuclear projects. However, in 2006, North Korea confirmed Bush's suspicions by testing a nuclear bomb. Tensions grew when North Korea sent a ballistic missile over Japan in September 2017. That same month, the North Koreans claimed to have detonated a hydrogen bomb. Arms races continue and the Doomsday Clock ticks.

"The days are gone forever when our enemies could blackmail us with nuclear bombs."

North Korean leader Kim Jong-Un, 2012

"We have a very robust and secure command-and-control system over our strategic nuclear assets."

Pakistan Prime Minister Shahid Khaqan Abbasi, 2017

◀ **Estimates suggest India has from 110 to 120 nuclear weapons, a few of which were on display during the annual Republic Day parade in Delhi in 2009.**

PERSPECTIVES

Who might put up signs like this one? How do they want people to feel about nuclear arms? Who is the intended audience? How does this sign compare to propaganda the Soviets created during the Arms Race?

▼ **Billboards in North Korea are used as propaganda to promote the nation's nuclear capabilities.**

ANALYZE THIS

What does this image reveal about India? Who are the four men, and what is the setting? What message does it give Indian citizens, and why?

TIMELINE

1917

1950

1965

1917 The Bolsheviks take control of Russia and create the world's first communist state

1938 Scientists discover nuclear fission

December 1941 The U.S. government launches the Manhattan Project to produce the first atomic bomb

December 2, 1942 Enrico Fermi and a team of scientists produce the first controlled chain reaction using nuclear fission

1943 Theoretical physicist J. Robert Oppenheimer takes charge of the Manhattan Project in Los Alamos, New Mexico

July 16, 1945 The United States tests the first atomic bomb in Alamogordo, New Mexico

August 6, 1945 United States drops the first atomic bomb on Hiroshima, Japan

August 9, 1945 President Truman issues orders to drop an atomic bomb on Nagasaki, Japan

November 1945 Manhattan Project scientists form the Federation of Atomic Scientists (FAS)

October 12, 1946 The Canadian government establishes the Atomic Energy Control Act

1947 President Truman unveils the Truman Doctrine to help contain communism

August 1949 The U.S.S.R. tests its first nuclear weapon, "First Lightning"

October 1952 Great Britain tests its first atomic weapon off the coast of Australia

November 1, 1952 The United States detonates the world's first hydrogen bomb, "Ivy Mike"

August 12, 1953 The U.S.S.R. tests its first thermonuclear device

November 22, 1955 The Soviets test their first true hydrogen bomb

1957 The Soviet Union launches the first satellite into space

1960 The Soviets shoot down a U.S. spy plane over Russia, bringing an end to disarmament talks

1960 France tests its first nuclear weapon

October 22, 1962 The Cuban missile crisis begins, lasting 13 days

August 5, 1963 The U.S., Soviet, and British governments sign the Limited Test Ban Treaty

1966

1969 Strategic Arms Limitation Talks (SALT) begin

1979 SALT II comes into effect

1987 President Reagan and Soviet premier Mikhail Gorbachev engage in talks to end the Arms Race

May 11, 1998 India detonates three massive nuclear weapons

2006 North Korea tests a nuclear bomb

March 2017 North Korea launches several missiles into waters off the coast of Japan, and the United States announces plans to build a missile defense system in South Korea

May 18, 1974 India tests its first atomic bomb

March 23, 1983 President Reagan announces the Strategic Defense Initiative (SDI)

December 25, 1991 Gorbachev resigns from his post and the U.S.S.R. is dissolved, bringing an end to the Cold War

December 2016 U.S. President-elect Donald Trump tweets plans to strengthen U.S. arsenal of nuclear weapons

September 2017 North Korea sends a ballistic missile over Japan and claims to have detonated a hydrogen bomb

2018

World map showing nuclear armed or nuclear capable states

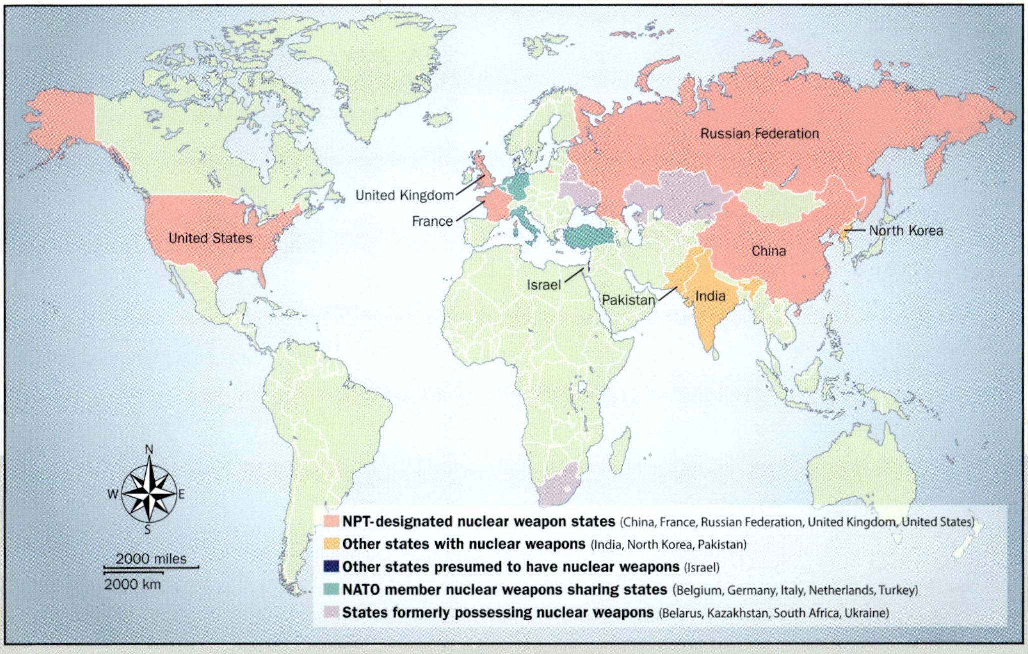

BIBLIOGRAPHY

QUOTATIONS

p. 4. Sagan, Carl. ABC News Viewpoint. *The Famous People, 2017.* https://quotes.thefamouspeople.com/carl-sagan-155.php

p. 6. King, Jr., Martin Luther. Nobel Prize lecture at the University of Oslo, December 11, 1964. "Martin Luther King, Jr. and the Struggle for Freedom." http://kingencyclopedia.stanford.edu/encyclopedia/quotes_contents.html

p. 8. Einstein, Albert. "Atomic Education Urged by Einstein," *The New York Times*, May 25, 1946. https://federalunion.org.uk/albert-einstein/

p. 10. Kennedy, John F. inaugural address, January 20, 1961. John F. Kennedy Quotations. www.jfklibrary.org/Research/Research-Aids/Ready-Reference/JFK-Quotations/Inaugural-Address.aspx

p. 14. Rotblat, Joseph. Joseph Rotblat: Nobel Lecture. Nobelprize.org, 2017. www.nobelprize.org/nobel_prizes/peace/laureates/1995/rotblat-lecture.html

p. 16. Kahn, Herman. *Thinking About the Unthinkable in the 1980s.* New York: Simon and Schuster, 1984.

p. 19. Kennedy, Robert. BrainyQuote.com, Xplore Inc, 2017. www.brainyquote.com/quotes/quotes/r/robertkenn746001.html

p. 20. Carter, Jimmy. BrainyQuote.com, Xplore Inc, 2017. www.brainyquote.com/quotes/quotes/j/jimmycarte453566.html

p. 23. Kissinger, Henry. *The Cycles of American History.* Arthur Meier Schlesinger. Houghton Mifflin Company, 1999.

p. 25. Bradley, Omar. *America Needs Human Rights.* Edited by Anuradha Mittal and Peter Rosset. Food First Books, 1999.

p. 27. Reagan, Ronald. "Best Reagan Quotes on Nuclear Weapons." The Reagan Vision for a Nuclear-Weapons-Free World, 2017. www.thereaganvision.org/quotes/

p. 28. Rabinowitch, Eugene. *The Bulletin of the Atomic Scientists.* http://www.wired.co.uk/article/what-is-the-doomsday-clock

p. 31. Russell-Einstein Manifesto. *Einstein: The First Hundred Years.* Edited by Maurice Goldsmith, Alan Mackay, and James Woudhuysen. Pergamon Press, 1980, p. 113.

p. 33. Churchill, William. "Winston Churchill and the Cold War." National Churchill Museum, 2017. www.nationalchurchillmuseum.org/winston-churchill-and-the-cold-war.html

p. 34. Oppenheimer, Julius Robert. "As Hiroshima Smouldered, Our Atom Bomb Scientists Suffered Remorse." Paul Ham. Newsweek, August 5, 2015.

p. 36. Dylan, Bob. "Bob Dylan on Old America and 'Modern' Times." Jann S. Wenner. Rolling Stone, May 3, 2007. www.rollingstone.com/music/news/bob-dylan-on-old-america-and-modern-times-20070503

p. 38. Putin, Vladimir. "Vladimir Putin Signals Renewal of Nuclear Arms Race: 'We are stronger now than anyone'." National Post, December 23, 2016. http://nationalpost.com/news/world/vladimir-putin-signals-renewal-of-nuclear-arms-race

p. 38. Trump, Donald. Twitter, Inc. twitter.com, 2017. https://twitter.com/realdonaldtrump/status/811977223326625792?lang=en

p. 40. Kim Jong-Un. "North Korean Leader Stresses Need for Strong Military." Choe Sang-Hun. *The New York Times,* April 15, 2012. www.nytimes.com/2012/04/16/world/asia/kim-jong-un-north-korean-leader-talks-of-military-superiority-in-first-public-speech.html

p. 40. Shahid Khaqan Abbasi. http://www.huffingtonpost.in/2017/09/20/pak-pm-says-have-developed-short-range-nuclear-weapons-to-counter-indias-cold-start-doctrine_a_23217318/

TO FIND OUT MORE

Fetter-Vorm, Jonathan. *Trinity: A Graphic History of the First Atomic Bomb*. New York: Hill & Wang, 2012.

Goldsmith, Connie. *Bombs Over Bikini: The World's First Nuclear Disaster.* Minneapolis, Minnesota: Lerner Publishing Group, 2014.

Mason, Dr. Jennifer. *The Nuclear Arms Race.* New York: Gareth Stevens, 2017.

Nakazawa, Keiji. *Barefoot Gen: A Cartoon Story of Hiroshima.* San Francisco: Last Gasp Books, 2004.

Dr. Seuss. *The Butter Battle Book.* New York: Random House for Young Readers, 2013.

Sheinkin, Steve. Bomb: The Race to Build—and Steal—the World's Most Dangerous Weapon. New York: Turtleback Books, 2015.

Tatsuta, Kazuto. *Ichi-F: A Worker's Graphic Memoir of the Fukushima Nuclear Power Plant*. New York: Kodansha Comics, 2017.

INTERNET GUIDELINES

Finding good source material on the Internet can sometimes be a challenge. When analyzing how reliable the information is, consider these points:

- Who is the author of the page? Is it an expert in the field or a person who experienced the event?
- Is the site well known and up to date? A page that has not been updated for several years probably has out-of-date information.
- Can you verify the facts with another site? Always double-check information.
- Have you checked all possible sites? Don't just look on the first page a search engine provides. Remember to try government sites and research papers.
- Have you recorded website addresses and names? Keep this data so you can backtrack and verify the information you want to use.

WEBSITES:

Ducksters Education Site
Learn all about major events in the Arms Race.
www.ducksters.com/history/cold_war/arms_race.php

John F. Kennedy Presidential Library and Museum
Find out about President Kennedy's role in the Cold War and the Arms Race.
www.jfklibrary.org/JFK/JFK-in-History/The-Cold-War.aspx

Library of Congress
View a collection of political cartoons about the Arms Race by Herbert Block.
http://www.loc.gov/collections/herblock-cartoon-drawings/about-this-collection/

Manhattan Project
National Parks Service resource about The Dawn of the Atomic Age.
www.nps.gov/mapr/index.htm

Canadian Civil Defense Museum
Find posters, political cartoons, and other source materials about the Arms Race.
http://civildefencemuseum.ca/

National Post
Learn how Canadians prepared for potential nuclear threats during the Cold War.
http://nationalpost.com/news/canada/this-is-a-real-emergency-chilling-artifacts-from-when-canada-prepared-for-nuclear-annihilation

CBC Digital Archives
Listen to an audio recording of women protesting nuclear testing in Canada.
www.cbc.ca/archives/entry/1962-voice-of-women-protests-nuclear-testing

Khan Academy
Find out how people felt about atomic weapons in the 1950s.
www.khanacademy.org/humanities/ap-us-history/period-8/apush-1950s-america/a/atomic-fears-and-the-arms-race

GLOSSARY

accurate Correct in all details

Allies Nations, such as Great Britain, France, Canada, the United States, and the Soviet Union, that fought together against Germany during World War II

analyze Examine closely

archives Places that store historical information about a location, a person, or an event

arsenal A collection of weapons and military equipment

artifact An object made by human beings

atmospheric Relating to Earth's atmosphere

atomic Relating to the energy produced by splitting atoms

auditory Related to the sense of hearing

Axis Powers The alliance of Germany, Italy, and Japan during World War II

balanced Judged or presented in a way that is fair and takes all views into account

biased Prejudiced in favor of or against one thing, person, or group

biomedical Relating to biology and medicine

campaigned Worked in an organized way to achieve a specific goal

catastrophic Causing a large amount of damage or suffering

centuries Periods of 100 years

civilian A person who is not a member of the armed forces or police force

classes Levels in society based on how much money, power, and status people have

classified Information or documents listed as officially secret and only accessible by authorized people

Cold War The worldwide political, economic, and military confrontation between the United States, the Soviet Union, and their allies that lasted from 1946 to 1991

communism An economic and political system in which all property is owned by its members and is used for the good of all people

confidential Private or secret

containment Keeping something under control

contamination The state of polluting or poisoning something

context The circumstances in which an event occurs

credentials Qualifications or achievements

credible Something that can be believed

culture The ideas, customs, and behavior of a people

democracy A political system in which government is made up of representatives elected by adult citizens

detonated Caused to explode

disarmament The reduction or elimination of military weapons

economy Creating, earning, and spending wealth

evacuated Removed from a dangerous place and sent somewhere safe

evidence The information or facts that indicate whether something is true or not

fascist A system of government that is led by a dictator who has complete power

hydrogen A chemical element consisting of an odorless, colorless, flammable gas

impartial Treating something equally or fairly

imperial Relating to an empire, or being under the supreme rule of a single supreme authority

intercontinental ballistic missiles Missiles that can be propelled more than 3,400 miles (5,472 km)

Manhattan Project A U.S. top-secret project that involved developing nuclear weapons for use during World War II

missiles Objects that are forcefully launched at targets

nuclear fission The process of splitting a heavy atomic nucleus into smaller parts with the release of energy

nuclear fusion The process of atomic nuclei fusing together with the release of energy

perspective Point of view or way of looking at things

primary sources Firsthand accounts or direct evidence of an event

propaganda Information, often misleading or biased, used to promote a particular point of view

radioactive fallout Material emitting radiation or nuclear energy that shoots into the atmosphere during a nuclear explosion then falls back to Earth

republics Governments in which the power lies in the ability for people to elect their head of state

retaliation The act of returning a military attack

sanctions Official permissions or approvals

satellite Humanmade object sent into orbit around bodies in space

secondary sources Materials created by studying primary sources

society A group of people forming a single community with its own distinctive culture and institutions

source materials Original documents or other pieces of evidence used by historians to learn about an event

spies People employed by a government or other organization to secretly obtain information about an enemy or competitor

thermonuclear Relating to nuclear reactions at high temperatures

treaties Agreements between nations

uranium A chemical element used to make nuclear energy

World War II War fought from 1939 to 1945 between the United States, Canada, Britain, the U.S.S.R., and their allies against Nazi Germany, Italy, Japan, and their allies: The United States, U.S.S.R., and Japan did not join until 1941.

INDEX